THE NATIONAL POETRY SERIES

The National Poetry Series was established in 1978 to ensure the publication of five poetry books annually through five participating publishers. Publication is funded by the Lannan Foundation; Stephen Graham; Joyce & Seward Johnson Foundation; Juliet Lea Hillman Simonds; The Poetry Foundation; and Olafur Olafsson.

2012 Competition Winners

the meatgirl whatever, by Kristin Hatch
of San Francisco, California
CHOSEN BY K. SILEM MOHAMMAD,
TO BE PUBLISHED BY FENCE B○

The Narrow Circle, by N⸱
of Chicago, Illi⸱.
CHOSEN BY DEAN YO
TO BE PUBLISHED BY PENGU.

The Cloud That Contained the Lightning, by ⸝ynthia Lowen
of Brooklyn, New York
CHOSEN BY NIKKY FINNEY,
TO BE PUBLISHED BY UNIVERSITY OF GEORGIA PRESS

Visiting Hours at the Color Line, by Ed Pavlić
of Athens, Georgia
CHOSEN BY DAN BEACHY-QUICK,
TO BE PUBLISHED BY MILKWEED EDITIONS

Failure and I Bury the Body, by Sasha West
of Austin, Texas
CHOSEN BY D. NURKSE,
TO BE PUBLISHED BY HARPERCOLLINS PUBLISHERS

THE CLOUD THAT
CONTAINED THE LIGHTNING

EST. 75 1938
YEARS
THE UNIVERSITY OF GEORGIA PRESS 2013

Cynthia Lowen

THE CLOUD THAT
CONTAINED THE LIGHTNING

The University of Georgia Press
Athens and London

Published by the University of Georgia Press
Athens, Georgia 30602
www.ugapress.org
© 2013 by Cynthia Lowen
All rights reserved
Designed by Kaelin Chappell Broaddus
Set in 10/14 Century Old Style
Printed and bound by Sheridan Books, Inc.
The paper in this book meets the guidelines for
permanence and durability of the Committee on
Production Guidelines for Book Longevity of the
Council on Library Resources.

Printed in the United States of America

13 14 15 16 17 P 5 4 3 2 1

Library of Congress Cataloging-in-Publication Data
Lowen, Cynthia.
[Poems. Selections]
The cloud that contained the lightning / Cynthia Lowen.
pages cm
Includes bibliographical references.
Poems.
ISBN-13: 978-0-8203-4564-2 (paperback : alk. paper)
ISBN-10: 0-8203-4564-4 (paperback : alk. paper)
I. Title.
PS3612.O8885C56 2013
811'.6–dc23
2013011986

British Library Cataloging-in-Publication Data available

For my mother and father

There is another theory of relativity, one more easily noticed and intuitively understood than Einstein's great theory. It speaks to human nature rather than to the nature of the physical universe, to the complementary relationship between observer and observed. It speaks to the occasional work in which an author comes to a deeper understanding of his own life through studying another.

J. ROBERT OPPENHEIMER

Contents

MATCH IN ONE HAND

THE ART OF SURRENDER

CLEAN HANDS

Acknowledgments

I would like to thank my grandfather, Irving S. Lowen, whose work on the Manhattan Project, and whose apprehension of the terrible power it would unleash, is where this all began.

I am grateful to my many teachers for their support, insight, and contagious love of poetry, including Jane Hilberry, David Mason, Stephen Dobyns, Marie Howe, and Ani Tuzman, who I still think of every time I hear chimes. And to Martha Rhodes, for your friendship, advice, and sense of humor through it all.

I am deeply indebted to the Fine Arts Work Center in Provincetown, Massachusetts, where most of these poems were written, for the invaluable gift of time, space, and community of kindred spirits. To those who generously read earlier drafts of this work, and whose thoughtful advice made it stronger, thank you.

To Nikky Finney, you are an inspiration. I am honored beyond words by your selection of this book for the National Poetry Series. I would also like to thank the University of Georgia Press.

And to my parents, my first and constant teachers, Ralph and Mary Ann.

Grateful acknowledgement goes out to the editors of the publications and anthologies in which some of these poems first appeared, occasionally in slightly different forms: *Best New Poets 2008, Black Warrior Review, Boston Review, Inkwell, Laurel Review, Provincetown Arts, A Public Space, Satellite Convulsions: Poems from* Tin House, and *Tin House.*

Oppenheimer Maps
His Coordinates

After so much time in the desert
I'm always finding myself at water.

The blue and bloated little men
point to the back of my head and warn,

You have no friends on that shore.

I collect them in a net
and probe them, my little cadavers.

Little brains, little hearts.
Mine—and cute, like the jarred fetal pig in biology class.

I made these.
They call me *father*.

FISSION

Atom

Greek for *átomos*, meaning the smallest
indivisible particle of matter.

The way violence makes an atom behave
like a drop of water,

the self casts a shadow of the self
moving in opposite directions.

Breakdown: passage from one state
to another. Water: neither ice nor cloud.

Indivisible, as in the smell of cut grass or single German words
that encompass entire moods. Schadenfreude:

the enjoyment we take from others' troubles.
Doppelganger: shadow self, harbinger of bad luck,

and schism.

Parable of the Children

Father they call him,
not meaning ours—

but ruler
of Titans,

last and most terrible offspring
of sky
and earth.

Cronos: who devoured his own brood
saying, *This is to protect you*
from becoming
like me.

Oppenheimer Wears
New Mexico as Camouflage

My two great loves are physics and New Mexico.
It's a pity they can't be combined.

J. ROBERT OPPENHEIMER

I confuse my heart
for the cactus fruit, covered in needles
and tasting like strawberries.

Each night one coyote is murdered,
and in the morning every dog is proud.

I am more bone
than blood. But where they meet,
blood will prevail.

The inconsequential mist on the mesa
reminds me of my skin.

I plan to disappear.

To the east is the place that means
Knowledge of Goodness.

To the west, the place that means
Defiance of the Knowledge of Goodness.

I stand on the bridge between them,

spitting into the river
that pries them apart.

Tea with the Wives Club

Tsk, says June, says, *look you great!*
Alice: *Hair great too your looks.*
Mary to Alice: *Your too great hair looks.* Imagine

June. One long, pink month.

Cake this love I. Offer more.

June is so in New Mexico lovely. June.

Miracle of water in the arroyo. Futile
sound of milk through a straw.

The blooming are cottonwood.
Species of tolerant poplar.

Lovely.
Lovely.
Lovely.

Without any practical value.

Designed to propagate
cotton seeds, cotton tadpoles
swimming across the mesa.

Get you where recipe did?
The flowers on June's dress, and the mouth
on her face,

want to pluck them—

And?

—and put them in a vase.

So we lucky are.
We are lucky so.
Lucky are so we.

Imagine riding Peter's toy train
through the wall. *Sigh.*

Where time does the go?
Where have I gone?
Lift a finger don't. Acquiesce.

This is so pleasant always.
Pleasant this always is so.
Always is this so pleasant.

June's wide, pink mouth,
a salmon that swallows
empty hooks.

Goodbye.
Goodbye.
Goodbye.

Oppenheimer Admires
the Prints of Hokusai

Always a great wave overcoming
the miniature people. Each face bears the same
expectation.

Mount Fuji will wait forever
for the seekers of high ground—

they meet the waves in boats, assuming
Mount Fuji will drown.

The wave you intended broods above
the blue wave. Sometimes, the sign for warning
escapes us.

Each lie contains two types of secrets:

the first is kept from others.
The second is kept from oneself.

Both waves will break
over the miniature people.

Oppenheimer Plays Risk
Wearing a Blindfold

Mongolia is under attack,
but I couldn't imagine that place
or why I should feel offended.

Someone traced a shape with my finger, saying, *Home,*
and so, being positive of one thing only,
I lined it with my armies.

(*Think of the whole board as yours.*)

I was given little plastic artillery.
I was supposed to attack.

The player to my right blew his nose.
The player to the left tapped his pen.

How long do you think you can wait?

Someone put the dice in my palm
and forced me to roll.

Proposition

Dear Frank,

I'm riding toward a place called Coyote, despite the fact
I hate the damn animals. Understand the name
Coyote as either warning or a way to keep paradise private—
in other words, irresistible—and besides, I'm bored
with everything else. Have I told you how the natives
look at me with dog eyes? Meaning they smell me coming
from a long way off. The shamans blow smoke in my direction
and chant what must be a funeral song when the wind blows it
back at them. All this by way of an invitation, brother, to come,
preferably with a carton of cigarettes. —Robert

TRINITY

The Scientific Method

Try bashing
your two fists
against your own head

until your ears ring
and you have given yourself

enough punishment,   because this is not about destruction
                                   but generation through methods
                                   associated with destruction . . .

For a moment you will reside
in the space cleaved

between the loathed
and that filled

with loathing,   out of which you will straighten your tie
                          and begin the work
                          with your four hands.

Every Mother Says
Her Child Is Special

but look, do the math.

Are they waving bye-bye
or are they rags filled with straw
my wife has stuck on the lawn
to scare away the birds?

Parable of the Children

We grew up confined
by the walls
of his stomach,

knowing the world outside
was mainly
smoke.

Which of us was he starving?

Or did Earth offer him
that little?

Food fell like diamonds

the living toss
into graves:

evidence
we had not yet arrived
in hell

but that the door to hell
hinges
on what is beautiful

by virtue
of its partnership
with light.

Where was our mother?

Where was one voice asking,

Whatever happened
to those children?

Bedding Down

Sometimes, when we are lying here,
I have the urge to pull my hand
from your breast, ball it into a fist,
and smash your near-unconscious

face. It's like the fear
of calling out
in a silent theater
during the most important
part of the play.

The audience turns in their seats,
the actors on stage pause,
and I'm dragged away.

I wanted to see the show
as much as I wanted to lie here
whispering, *Love.*

Risk/Benefit

If this weapon does not persuade men of the need for
international collaboration and the need to put an end
to war, nothing that comes out of a laboratory ever will.

J. ROBERT OPPENHEIMER

If your job is to spare, mine is to squander,
to waste whole afternoons watching tumbleweeds succumb to wind
so that you may be relieved to discover how little one life is worth.

Let's play chicken—
I extend my arm out the window and you swerve at mailboxes
until we all understand the stakes: my job is to crack, splinter, and
    burst

and yours is to break my arm or pull off this road and return
to the woods you used to call
heaven. The actual woods. The actual peace.

And So What If We
Blow Up the Atmosphere?

Had a dog, liked to pitch its jaw over the cat asleep on the settee,
not biting down,
just pinning it there between the tepee of its teeth
and the upholstery—

rather than ponder the dog's demented plan for that cat
who must have come to think,
Get it over with already,

we'd pride ourselves, my family, tell people,
Damndest dog, fucking with the cat like that
but not *eating* it,

as if it said something about our moral compass, our *values* so
    highfalutin'
even our pets violated their instinct to kill—
like we were *special.*

Theories of Relativity

I prayed for a brother. Then I made up a language
to exclude him.

The reason for the heart's two chambers:

deceit as proof
of the heart's allegiance
to itself.

His idiotic faith in my goodness
made me good. I hid in the cupboard of his belief
with my porkpie hat and my pipe,

while the heart typed out its two-tongued correspondence.

I did not want a brother. I wanted to prove
there was a God. It was an experiment
I could never replicate.

Why Does Daddy Wear Sunglasses at Night?

Think of daddy like a fireman, in reverse, or no more like
an angel—no no—like God
the night God said,
Let there be light.

And Our Tracks Turned to
Glass in the Desert

and I thought, Hunh, now look at that
transmigration
of soles.

Remember the time we visited Dinosaur State Park?
Evidence of our own
lost species.

What to extrapolate from our stupid impractical shoes?

How fast did we run?
Where did we go?

Morning after Trinity;
or, Oppenheimer Wakes
and Remembers the
Woman of His Dreams

All ass: two hemispheres of flesh,
which were also, in the way of that world, scoops of ice cream
that would melt when I reached out my spoon.

This morning my wife is not my wife,
and I shave with a sense of naughtiness
while the birds sing, *Cheat-cheat, cheat-cheat.*

Both worlds being equal, I fear the alchemy of my razor
and the poached eggs set before me
with their little scarlet specks of potential.

Oppenheimer on the Couch

First, meaning possession.

Now, we have on our hands
this porcupine.

I chase it under the bed and dream
I'm a passenger on a doomed
cruise. The subconscious

has not been warned
about the use of cliché:

Sinking ship, it says.

Sometimes I want to steal,
but my understanding of loss prevents me.

Rock between two hard places.

We drowned in our teacups
and woke
on a bed of quills.

First, meaning option

not to use,
only wield.

MATCH IN ONE HAND

Oppenheimer at the
Natural History Museum

where squaws pound corn while thonged men turn bucks they
    scored on the rotisserie–
as if the Navajo fit the same class as the wooly mammoth across the
    hall,
extinct since the Holocene. Really. It's so offensive.

Like they're not still out here, selling rugs by the side of the road,
    cutting the urge
to shake the marbles from my eyes,
melt that grin off the wife's wax face,

rip off my pants to reveal a pink mound
where my cock should be:
a scene from the story on the plaque outside
explaining what the hell happened to us.

Notes from the Target Committee

I. TOKYO

Tokyo is a possibility, but it is now practically
all bombed and burned out . . .
THE TARGET COMMITTEE

Here, white shadow of Meiji Street,
here, white shadow of what was formerly called
the center, metastasizing up the vein

of the Onagi River. The reconnaissance photos return
x-rays of a doomed lung
from thirty-two thousand feet,

white heads of cauliflower
blooming from the cavity,
tissue aggregating tissue,

tumors of white fire against the black
negative. Invasive vegetable,
breaking off, re-rooting

in the liver, the brain, Yokohama,
Nagoya, island of terminal
shadows, rifled, run through

the CAT for one unspoiled
organ over which a different shadow
might fall.

Oppenheimer Finds a
Message in a Bottle

Petals from the *molotoffano hanakago*–
Molotov flower baskets–fall like a sign
someone is listening.

My father planted each stone in our garden
as if he were planting himself,
and now the red Molotov blossoms
scar their surface.

My father spent so much time in heaven
the earth became a mystery.

I peek through his hedge
to the real garden, where perhaps, after all,
we're not winning.

Notes from the Target Committee

II. KYOTO

I don't want Kyoto bombed.

SECRETARY OF WAR HENRY L. STIMSON

Breaking the spirit
is not ruining

          completely

but preserving a temple

to return to:
model on which the rubble

will be compelled again
toward sky

not as temples
but proof

defeat
is only reiterated

by second incarnations.

The spirit breaks
with the knowledge

of the choice—

that the monuments
paving the infinite dirt road
to enlightenment

were admired—

match in one hand
prayer in the other.

Oppenheimer Sends a
Message in a Bottle

Two seeds and instructions:
press deep into the soft, spring dirt—

by August the vines' dark scrawl
will shade your paper houses.

The bells bloom for a single morning
and fall by the afternoon. Do not mourn

the one flower—many will follow,
perennial, returning year again,

so that you won't forget me,
how I drank this wine

and launched my craft, drunk with conviction
it would find the appropriate party.

Where Can You Hide
a Think like That?

But people are so stupid, really,
and I don't care what you tell them:
tomorrow they will know

or tomorrow they will no longer
know a goddamn
thing. Same difference.

Sometimes I almost try to feel bad for them,
the *general population*,
thumbing through their almanacs advising,
Today's the best day to castrate animals.

Well. At least they got *that* right.

Notes from the Target Committee

III. HIROSHIMA

That no passing cloud
intervened. And the earth did not quake

to say, *Enough.*

That thirst, which earthly bodies
succumb to. And the sun was a fever

not to be taken personally. And the rose

was not to blame
for the thorn's perversion.

That the spirit collected dirt
beneath its fingernails.

That the spirit appealed to the moon's
blank face, feeling no sense

of communion.

That exhaustion, which earthly bodies
admit to.

And women wept into their scarves
to later meet a shadow there.

And the crowd
cheered. And the crowd

found excuse
for their ordinary failures

seeing it was not
an empire.

Hibakusha

Sardines
was the one game
the missionaries brought

for some higher
purpose

evincing the little coffin-
shaped can

and the church key
with which they exhumed

the neat rows of bodies
lined up fin
to fin

as if a whole school
had neatly
and with perfect order

swam in there
of their own
volition.

We counted to one hundred
while the boy we all loved most
was designated *It,*

sent off to find a coffin
we could join him in,

and we arrived
one by one—
a whole school of us.

Quantum Mechanics

I tried to pass through her like a ghost through a wall
and succeeded. I found the smallest part of the wall

and made myself smaller. I watched her brush her hair
and thought of all the women, at that moment, brushing their hair—

wanting to yank a whole handful from her head
so she'd tell me what a prick I am.

Notes from the Target Committee
IV. NAGASAKI

At Nagasaki there was a thick overcast . . .
then, at the last moment a hole in the clouds
appeared, permitting visual bombing.

GENERAL LESLIE R. GROVES

Sometimes I hate you
for not stopping me
from hurting you,

says the hurricane
inside the eye

where dandelions momentarily display
perfect white afros.

On the Doppler
a red cornea haloes
the steel blue iris,

and the weatherman warns,

Suspect any day shaped
like a donut

where only the hole
is habitable.

When the hurricane wants to believe itself,
it says,

I'm better now,

as if just by saying so
it might dissipate

into a front
that passed last week.

Inside the eye
bruises are storms
by another woman's name,

which the short memory forgets
because it has to.

Out on the lawn
dandelions hold their heads
like glasses on a tray

and the pinhole of sky
is wide as the picture

the mind takes
of a place it wants to remember.

Sometimes I think
we could live
like this

forever, says the hurricane,

reaching out
two fingers of wind
to pluck the first white seed.

What's War Got to Do with It?

Now we've got sliced bread; the sandwich is in vogue.

Parable of the Children

Not because we were wanted but because it's lonely being married

to the keeper
of human time,

our mother retrieved us to the world:

not the place
we'd left

—where the gods enjoyed
what they failed to recognize

as a golden age—

but the one we'd been warned about.

The story of the father is never the story of the ingenious
inventions by which the father hopes

to be fondly
remembered,

but the one where, in spite of all precaution,
man is circuitously destroyed

by his own
creations.

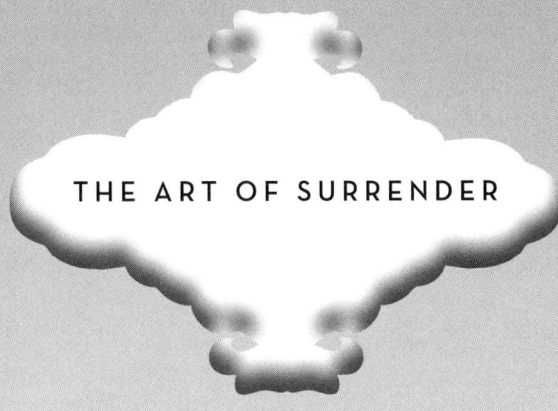

THE ART OF SURRENDER

The Wizard of Oz

In Kansas they are dreaming wickedness appears
as the archetype
of wickedness.

That's not "me"
but the spirit's malevolent pilot

pinning you against the refrigerator
insisting,

You're no good,
or,
You're not good
enough.

I want to say all bodies flow toward a natural valley
of kindness,

but they don't.

Out in the field, hives lean
like houses dropped by a twister,

and I'm the voice behind the veil—
giant brain, monster, ball of fire,

or the ordinary man.

Oppenheimer Studies
the Art of Surrender

Aphrodisiac, they say, oysters, the way we crack
their lids off while alive, unzip all at once
the salty sea and pulp, tip nacre to lip, and slurp

them up quick and whole, almost missing that life
as it glides over tongue. I thought muscle might hold
the hinge shut. I suffered a lack

of imagination or, rather, the unlikely hope
some pearl, some tough kernel
might keep the mouth from completing its advantage.

Such bad foresight, nature, failing to anticipate
the fisherman's prying fingers and the shucking knife wedged
between the shell that becomes a comb
and the shell that will be a button.

Hibakusha

Not corn but husk, our bed. I slip between
the paper sheets. The hair on my skin like corn silk.
The hair that was hers. That I peeled back from the kernel
of her face every morning   and kissed. Her body
of little seeds, bursting between my teeth.
Tore off the husk and said, *This is the best thing*
about summer. Roasted on coals, steamed from inside.
And the corn silk burned black as our hair. We said,
This is the best thing about losing our bodies. We were big
as the cloud of smoke, finally as big as we felt.
We burned our fingers picking ears from the fire.
Every summer I said, *This is the best crop.* Until it was.
We chose the right day to go down to the field and harvest.
She said the rows made a prison. I said, a cradle.
Once she had left the body, I knew she wouldn't return.
Hot, high summer. Sweet kernels. Picked just in time.

Principles of Uncertainty

As a boy I wanted to be good, loved
cotton candy and mother more than anyone,
wanted to please, and now may I say
I have squandered my sugar. I lick

and lick the bare cone,
but I'm a bad boy, mother, I've fucked
it up good, though you probably know that already,

what with all your new heavenly companions
who drink tea and wear thin
their mourning kimonos.

My only pain being your lipstick kissed
into the white linen napkin I saved
and thereby understand by multiplying

your lips, and I'm a bad, I'm a bad,
and I miss the snow on the rain on
the green grass on the great lawn I recently had

paved over—so as to avoid being reminded
of picnics or the smell of burning
leaves or your fingers tying on my hat
so I wouldn't catch cold while I made angels.

The Geology of
Brotherly Love

Rock cleaved to reveal
a grove of amethyst

thriving within
the violated night
representing a truer

nature:
who needs to be convinced
when you say,
I love you?

That which is ruled by laws
forcing disparate molecules

to hoard the same
electron

loves only the understanding
of how the world
works.

Inside the purple core
of the rock

silicone
and oxygen
bond not to each other

but to the spark
that passed between them

as we touched
holding our mother's
opposing hands.

It is not for love
that the molecules
fused into purple thorns,

simply
that two problems
could be solved
with the same answer

again
and again.

Building a House for the Boat

Kitty drank with an abandon
that was disturbing to watch.

JENNET CONANT, *109 EAST PALACE*

Wanted sails and a ceiling high enough—

the bed is an island,
the kitchen table is an island

cropping up like atolls
in the otherwise open sea.

I can't help wanting the fish to say something.
I want to say things.

Are we the people on the boat

floating from bed to kitchen table
and back again? Or are we
the boat

cresting the children like little waves
when they fall

overboard?

Oppenheimer Gets
Caught in a Blizzard

The tree does not look for mercy,
each needle tipped with stars of cold.

I used to believe
in a kind of relationship.

If I asked to be saved,
I would be.

When I thought the sky was listening,
I asked not to be held

accountable.

I watched the cloud that contained the lightning
unable to choose its target.

A dust devil picked sagebrush like a lice comb

and the dirt smelled so good I licked it
off the back of my hand . . .

The horizon is a lever hoisting the line
we have crossed. The horizon

has crushed its own fulcrum.

Each six-pointed star is different
and perfect. To say otherwise
is a sin.

It takes many stars to fill the valley,
and the valley is brimming.

When I thought the sky was listening,
I asked to be held.

CLEAN HANDS

Half-Life

Inside the unstable heart:
one little red suitcase

emptied
sock by unpaired
sock

until it is called
something else,
lighter

by loss—
how the feeling
of loss

crosses
like a full eclipse
behind which

you are forced
to turn out
every single
pocket

and become
your last
resurrection—

until
they call you
lead.

Tea Ceremony

It isn't that I don't feel bad; it is that I don't
feel worse tonight than I did last night.

J. ROBERT OPPENHEIMER,
UPON HIS FIRST VISIT TO JAPAN

At least we can communicate in bows.
At least we have clean cups, clean tea,
clean hands.

My server's cheeks remind me of a saddle—
plains of skin stretched
over pommel,
over horn. Or a figure

eight, sign for
infinity. In the body

I must be mindful of how I take each sip,
I must contemplate the silence of falling water.

Ichi-go ichi-e, they say.
For this time only, never again, one chance
in a lifetime.

I cannot hear the silence of falling water.
I do not want the other life
in this life.

My server bows to me.
I have brought that life to her.

Hibakusha

I never knew how to become what you loved.

I loved that dress, and now I wear it on my skin
forever. I had forgotten the war,

though I was still wearing the dress
I wore to school that day. I seeded

a garden. I was not a victim. I licked rice from my fingers
and watched koi kiss the surface of the pond.

The garden pushed up against my dress.
My dress was filled with wildflowers,

I thought. I forgot where I'd planted the seeds
until they bloomed. They were called

disgrace. We were not victims. I forgot the war.

Where Cancers Begin

for J.S.

Summer.
The grass they say cries
after cutting

mends itself,
persisting

along with the false assumption
that this is where circles begin: sand between our toes and the
    green lawns
begging to be mowed again, feeling

invincible. A cat's one outstretched paw
allows the mouse
to scuttle

undisturbed
but never

out of range, tracking
while at the same time
languishing—

sure of its claws
as the crabgrass
quietly hooking its barbed roots

far below the sod. In war,
cease-fires are only seasons
one side mistakes for peace,

the back of your hand
up and down my arm
wondering, *How so soft?*

forgetting or maybe just
not minding

your cells proliferating
their defenses.

You don't say you're dying,
and I don't name the children
you tell me we'll have some day,

perhaps the same one
the holy dirt they've been digging out behind the church
at Chimayo, New Mexico,

will mix with rainwater
and dust will become again
the man.

Meanwhile,
two kids are shot Good Friday morning
in the last miles of their pilgrimage—

trowels and a prayer in their back pocket
that God permit the suffering

one miracle,

and who's to say
He didn't?

Parable of the Children

And they live untouched by sorrow in the islands
of the blessed . . . and Cronos rules over them.

HESIOD, *WORKS AND DAYS*

If it is better to be feared
than loved, best of all

pitied.

At last it was Elysium,
pleasant corner of the underworld,

where, in his dotage,
we retired him.

So that he wouldn't feel diminished
by the fact war goes on

without him,

we crowned him king
of the virtuous

whose journey to that place was brief enough to believe
the pink blossoms of asphodel

are still precious
in their capacity to die.

Oppenheimer Finds a Lover;
or, Afternoon at the Shore

I take the canoe in rough water.
I go when the black afternoon
storms come in, as they do, most days.

I lower myself in the prow, lie down
with the woman whose body will never be found.
That one looks like an umbrella,

and this one, look, a bell. She gives the same cloud
many names. Out of consideration
she never says, *Mushroom.*

I try to give her reasons but the ocean
interrupts. It makes excuses for me.
Oh but really, how could I blame you?

After the Clouds Pass; or, Meditation on the Banks of the Lethe

For fuckssake, I've got house plants lived longer than some folks,
and you expect me to feel
bad?

Like rivers, my friend. People. Drain out one place.
Pick up in another.

Notes

"Oppenheimer Admires the Prints of Hokusai": Hokusai, a renowned artist and printmaker of the Edo period, is best known for the series "Thirty-Six Views of Mount Fuji," which includes the iconic print *The Great Wave off Kanagawa*.

"Hibakusha": This Japanese word, which is the title to several poems in the book, translates literally to *explosion-affected people* and is the term widely used in Japan to refer to victims of the atomic bombings of Hiroshima and Nagasaki.

"Notes from the Target Committee": The Target Committee consisted of military and scientific personnel, including J. Robert Oppenheimer, tasked with assembling a list of "favorable" target sites in Japan for the use of an atomic bomb, based on criteria including psychological factors, weather conditions, military strongholds, and which urban areas had been spared previous bombings so that the effects of an atomic blast could be studied.

"Where Cancers Begin": The church at Chimayo, New Mexico, is one of the oldest missions in the United States, where thousands of pilgrims come every year to retrieve healing earth out of a small hole in the ground in one of the antechambers. In April 2000 two teenagers were shot and killed on Good Friday morning en route to the church.